10 9 8 7 6 5 4 3 2 1 LIFTOFF!

THE PREGNANCY BOOK FOR MEN

KNOCK KNOCK®
VENICE, CALIFORNIA

Originally published in Dutch by Uitgeverij Snor
© 2009 Uitgeverij Snor
All rights reserved
Published in English by Who's There Inc.
Venice, CA 90291
knockknockstuff.com

Edited translation © 2014 Who's There Inc.
All rights reserved
Knock Knock is a trademark of Who's There Inc.
Made in China

The rights to this book have been negotiated by the literary agency
Sea of Stories, www.seaofstories.com

Concept by Uitgeverij Snor
Original text by Gerard Janssen
Original editing by Suzanne de Boer
Design and artwork by Job, Joris & Marieke, www.jobjorisenmarieke.nl

ISBN: 978-160106654-1
UPC: 82570331055-9

10 9 8 7 6 5 4 3 2

CONTENTS

PREFACE

When my girlfriend was pregnant the first time, I found reading her pregnancy books fascinating. Every week there would be a little story about what was happening to the baby and "you." But that "you" wasn't "me." Those texts were not written for me. *You're probably feeling sick . . . A stabbing pain or upset stomach; don't worry. It all comes with the territory.* I did not have stabbing pains and I did not have an upset stomach. Or if I did, it was for less exciting reasons. In any case, I did not want to know how it felt to be pregnant; I wanted to know how it worked. How does a fertilized egg become a living being? What is DNA? What is a chromosome? But nobody talked about that.

Now, after three pregnancies, I understand the tone of those pregnancy books much better. My emotional development is about ten years behind that of the average woman, and I'm guessing the same goes for other men. When I look back at that first pregnancy, I realize how bad I was at grasping what pregnancy means to a woman. How much she has invested in it, and how profound her worries are. And not just about the baby inside of her, but also about that loud-mouth who keeps making jokes about the pregnancy calendar, and who's supposed to become a "real" dad.

So here's a pregnancy book for men. On the one hand, it has somewhat masculine—or, more precisely, nerdy—stories about the machinery of pregnancy and the nature of life. On the other hand, it has some explanations of what your partner is going through. Because she's changing as well. She doesn't laugh at your jokes anymore, and she no longer thinks it's cool if you want to climb Mount Everest. That's why it doesn't hurt to teach a dad-to-be some "pregnant-woman things." If I could, I would travel back in time about ten years and give myself some good tips. Of course, that's not possible, but I did manage to make this little book.

Gerard Janssen

Nine Months or Forty Weeks?

A pregnancy takes nine months. But what is nine months? Some months have 30 days, others have 31, and February usually only has 28. This, of course, does not mean that a pregnancy is shorter when you get pregnant in February. To make matters easier, we usually express pregnancies in weeks. An average pregnancy takes forty weeks. But don't forget: when the doctor says the pregnancy is "in week 8," it actually means the embryo is six weeks old. The doctor starts counting from the first day of your partner's menstrual period just before she got pregnant.

A woman usually does a pregnancy test in the fifth week of the pregnancy, when the embryo is three weeks old and she's one week late. Are you keeping up? No worries if not. We'll start this book at the moment that makes the most sense—the fertilization. After all, the book is intended for men. But, just to avoid confusion, we'll follow the doctors' way of counting, and call the fertilization week 3. And by the way, we follow Mayo Clinic's method for dating trimesters, but other sources may vary by a week or two.

the 1st TRIMESTER!

The beginning and the end of the first trimester are milestones in a pregnant woman's life. The beginning, because that's when she finds out that she's pregnant. And the end, because from then on there's a reduced chance of miscarrying.

The Little One

You've just experienced one of the most important moments of your life, and you have pushed, either on purpose or by chance, the first domino of something that is far beyond your imagination. Whatever you may have been up to, one way or the other, up to 200 of your sperm reached your partner's egg. One of them was a direct hit and managed to find a way through the egg's wall. The egg was fertilized, and cell division has started. Blub . . . blub . . . blub . . . The blob is coming to life.

The Big One

Within forty-eight hours of fertilization, a woman's body starts producing a protein called EPF (short for early pregnancy factor) that ensures her immune system does not reject the embryo. But none of this is visible on the outside. Your partner is behaving in a normal manner. For now, that is. You two are probably watching TV casually, while magical processes are going on inside her belly.

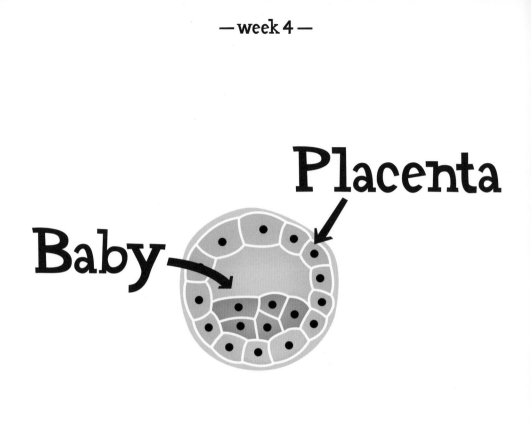

Baby **Placenta**

The Little One

After a series of cell divisions over five to six days, the blob becomes a sphere known as a blastocyst. The inner two layers of this ball will become the baby, while the outer layer will become the placenta and amniotic sac. (See also "The Chicken and the Egg," page 107.) Somewhere between six and twelve days after fertilization, the blastocyst will produce the hormone hCG (human chorionic gonadotropin), which is a key player in the hormonal symphony of early pregnancy.

The Big One

HCG

leads to the production of progesterone, which in turn leads to the growth of small blood vessels in the wall of the uterus, helping the fertilized egg to settle in comfortably. HCG also creates typical pregnancy signs such as morning sickness. A pregnancy test reacts to the presence of this hormone. From this moment on, a pregnancy test will indicate that your partner is pregnant.

THE
FIRST
CHECKUP

When your partner is pregnant, you'll get to meet some new people—for example, the doctor. You may also meet a midwife, and possibly even a doula. A doula is a kind of pregnancy/birth coach who will tell your partner that she's doing great and that she should have others (yes, that means you) spoil her.

Plastic Uterus

The first prenatal doctor visit often takes place around week 8. And you'd better have a very good reason if you're not going to be there, if only to get an early introduction to the magical world of childbirth.

On the walls of the doctor's office you may see dozens of birth announcements or artistic impressions of mothers with babies. There may also be a plastic uterus with a plastic fetus somewhere. Additionally, you may see all kind of electrical equipment next to the exam bed. As long as you don't touch anything or make any jokes, you really can't do too much harm.

Intimate Questions

The doctor may ask some intimate questions, including questions about menstruation, past pregnancies or abortions, family medical history, and even drug use or domestic violence. It's all important information for the doctor, so make sure to support your partner in being honest and forthcoming—even if that means offering to leave the room for a bit.

At this visit, the doctor will also determine the due date and give your partner a physical exam, and will take or order several blood and urine tests. She may also discuss testing for fetal abnormalities. These tests can include ultrasound, amniocentesis and chorionic villus sampling (which are both invasive), and the newer, noninvasive blood tests, which can also determine the baby's gender. Depending on how far along she is, your partner may also receive her first ultrasound, in which case you may get your first glimpse of the baby's heartbeat.

Heartbeat

After the first visit, there are about four weeks until the next visit. Often the highlight of this second visit is witnessing the baby's heartbeat—either seeing it on an ultrasound or hearing it with a Doppler instrument, a special kind of microphone. This can be an emotional moment, and surprising, too: the heartbeat may sound like a panting dog or galloping horse.

Doctor visits will be scheduled about every four weeks through the second trimester. Later in the third trimester they will become more frequent, and at the very end will be weekly. The doctor will monitor your partner's health and well-being, and she'll monitor the baby's development, too. Every visit, she'll check your partner's blood pressure and the baby's heartbeat. She'll also measure its growth and check its position.

Ultrasound

An ultrasound machine projects inaudible sound waves off tissues in the pregnant woman's abdomen, creating a blurred image of the baby inside her. These images are visible on a kind of television screen. Between weeks 8 and 12 an ultrasound is performed, among other things, to measure the embryo's length, which helps the doctor to determine its age and due date.

At around weeks 18 to 20, a more detailed ultrasound (sometimes called a "structural" ultrasound) is performed to check the fetus's development and determine whether there's enough amniotic fluid. The most important reason for this screening is to check for visible congenital or structural defects.

This screening ultrasound has advantages and disadvantages. Advantage: it's a medical test, and lets you check numerous things. When everything is in order, it's great to see how your child is developing. You can learn its sex, see how much the baby has grown, if it already sucks its thumb, or likes to kick. Disadvantage: your child could have a defect—information that is helpful to learn but certainly not easy to hear. Additionally, the doctor might believe she sees something off—which may or may not turn out to be the case. This may cause unnecessary stress. Finally, it's good to keep in mind that the doctor can't see everything, and might miss a problem that does exist.

Prenatal Screening

Nowadays, there are several prenatal tests that can be conducted to see if there is anything wrong with the baby. You actually take these tests in order to be told that nothing is wrong. If something *is* wrong, you will have to deal with some difficult dilemmas. Note: testing may vary from state to state, so be sure to check with your doctor about protocols in your area.

Rhesus Factor

There are four different blood types: A, B, AB, and O. Additionally, there is the Rhesus factor + or -. So you can have blood type O+, the most common blood type, or AB-, the most uncommon blood type. About fifteen percent of people in the US have a negative blood type. If your partner has a negative Rhesus factor and you have a positive one, there could be problems. If the baby's blood turns out to be positive and enters the mother's bloodstream, she will produce antibodies against the Rhesus positive blood, which may be bad for the baby. If this is her first pregnancy, the concern is not as great as in subsequent pregnancies.

If your partner is Rhesus negative and has not started producing antibodies to your baby's blood, she will receive an Rh immune globulin injection around week 28, just to make sure. This injection will ensure that she does not create antibodies. She should also receive this injection after giving birth if the baby is Rhesus positive, to ensure that during a following pregnancy no issues will arise. This is not necessary if your baby is Rhesus negative.

First Trimester Screening

First trimester screening is conducted between weeks 11 and 14. This screening consists of two tests: a blood test, to check whether certain substances are present in the blood; and an ultrasound scan, which measures the space at the back of the neck of the fetus (an NT scan, or nuchal translucency scan). A calculation can be made to determine the chance that the baby will have Down syndrome. If an increased chance of Down's is indicated, the mother can have follow-up testing, which can include one of the newer noninvasive maternal blood tests; amniocentesis; or chorionic villus sampling (CVS). Whatever the results may be, there's always a risk of having a baby with Down syndrome.

Noninvasive Prenatal Testing

Noninvasive prenatal screening blood tests (MaterniT21, Harmony, etc.) gauge the likelihood of certain chromosomal abnormalities in the fetus by testing the mother's blood. This is possible because the mother's blood contains a small amount of DNA from the fetus. Likewise, these tests are able to determine the baby's sex and blood type.

Women may prefer these blood tests since they pose no risk of miscarriage and are considered highly reliable. In addition, they can be performed as early as the tenth week of pregnancy. However, depending on your partner's age and situation, they may not be recommended by her doctor or covered by her insurance.

Chorionic Villus Sampling (CVS)

The advantage of the CVS test is that it can be conducted early, usually between 10 and 12 weeks. The disadvantage is that it cannot detect neural tube defects, and carries a higher risk of miscarriage than amniocentesis. For the CVS test, the doctor will use a needle to remove a small piece of tissue from the placenta. The tissue will be cultured and its DNA studied. In rare cases, CVS results are ambiguous, which may mean a follow-up amniocentesis.

Amniocentesis

Amniocentesis is usually done after week 15. The doctor uses a needle to extract some amniotic fluid through the abdominal wall. Screening of the amniotic fluid may indicate if the baby has a chromosomal or DNA abnormality. Possible metabolic disorders, spina bifida, or anencephaly will also come to light.

Quad Test

Quad screening is a maternal blood test performed between weeks 14 and 22 that gauges the likelihood of chromosomal or neural tube abnormalities in the fetus. False-positive results are fairly common with this test, requiring follow-up testing.

actual size

The Little One

The embryo is now a little pear about as big as a sesame seed, consisting of three layers: ectoderm, endoderm, and mesoderm. From the ectoderm, the brain, nervous system, skin, and nails will be created, among other things (see also "Brain Development," page 81). The mesoderm is the early stage of the heart, blood cells, skeleton, kidneys, and muscles. The endoderm will develop into the lungs, airways, and the digestive tract.

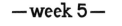

The Big One

Oftentimes, this is the week of the pregnancy test. Chances are your partner will utter weird sounds when she reads the results. She may be very happy, not happy at all, or both at the same time. Chances are you will be dumbfounded, will not know what to feel, and will not know what to do. You may be staring at the two lines like a zombie as your brain activity shuts down. You'll probably start pacing around the room or rocking back and forth in your chair. You may get up to make a drink to toast the moment, only to get to the kitchen and forget why you're there.

If you're the type of man who likes to approach his loved one from behind and hold her breasts when you don't know what to do, you should realize that her breasts may be extra sensitive. It can never hurt to explain to her that men often do not know what to say to express their feelings. Men often translate their feelings into physical, annoying, or even childish behavior. Sometimes women confuse the male way of showing emotions with insensitivity.

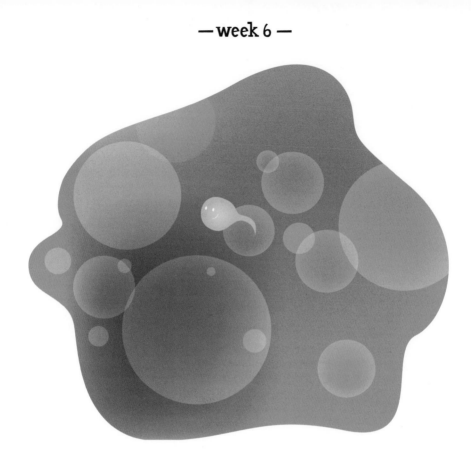

The Little One

It's a good thing that you can't see the embryo yet, or you might doubt that it's yours. Right now it's around a quarter of an inch long, and resembles a mutant tadpole. The embryo is already starting to develop little stumps where the arms and legs will be, though. The neural tube is closing (see page 82 for more info), the eyes and ears are also beginning to develop, and the heart has begun to beat.

The Big One

You may as well forget about inviting friends over at night for now. And don't get any big ideas about life after 8 p.m. A pregnant woman can be unbelievably tired in the evening. She'll appreciate you adapting to the situation and showing you're a sweet homebody. Curl up on the couch together and go to bed early. If you want to keep the atmosphere at home nice and pleasant, make sure you don't stay at work too late. And make sure you eat healthy. You may want to ask casually if she has already made an appointment with the doctor and if she's taking folic acid and vitamin D, preferably in the form of a complete prenatal vitamin. (Folic acid is essential for the development of the fetus, and vitamin D may prevent gestational diabetes, preeclampsia, and premature labor.) Also, it sounds very sympathetic if you ask such questions.

The Little One

The embryo is not quite half an inch long from crown to rump, which is how they measure babies during most of their time in the womb. Last week daddy's little one was only a funny little tadpole, but now it's starting to look like a real baby. An alien baby, perhaps, with a big square head, but still a baby with arms and legs. (And, sure, the hands look more like flippers.) The nose, mouth, eyes, brain, and kidneys are also developing nicely.

The Big One

If you have cats, from now on you'll be Head Cat Litter Remover. Cat poop may contain toxoplasma, a parasite that causes toxoplasmosis. Everything will be just fine as long as you start cleaning the cat box and washing your hands afterwards. In any case, it may be a good thing if you start taking care of the cats. The relationship between women and their cats often changes after a baby is born. This means that it deteriorates. By the way, toxoplasma (and many other disgusting things) may also appear in raw meat, so women are advised against eating steak (or any other meat) that's not well cooked. And while we're on the subject, it's better for your lady friend to also refrain from eating raw dairy products (which may carry *salmonella*, *E. coli*, and *listeria*).

The Little One

This week, the embryo is about a half-inch long. The little brain is developing like crazy, and lungs are beginning to form. The tiny arms and legs are getting longer, and at the end of the arms the flippers are starting to develop into fingers. The baby is also starting to move a bit.

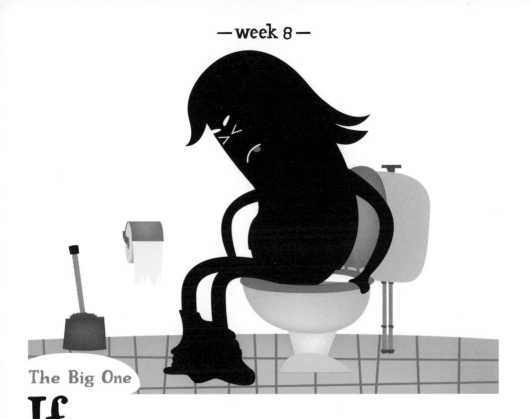

The Big One

If your partner has not yet suffered any sickness or other feelings of misery, then chances are that this is the week they will start to kick in. Especially in the morning, a pregnant woman can feel pretty miserable, with a runny nose, headaches, nausea, and vomiting. During the day she may start feeling better (though for some women, "morning sickness" really happens at night). Try to spoil her a bit. Lots of fluids and many little snacks, even if she feels sick, usually help to ease the suffering. Another well-known problem with pregnant women is constipation. All of a sudden she may start to worry about how she'll deliver a baby when she can't even go to the bathroom. Try to remain serious and understanding. By the way, if she doesn't experience any problems, it's no reason for concern. Some women feel just fine during this phase.

WHAT IS LIFE?

Many women will change irreversibly when they're pregnant, finding that they can no longer stand a mess. Chances are, you're a guy who associates messy surroundings with comfort and liveliness. So it's a good idea to stop and think for a minute about what "life" actually is. It may help you understand why housework matters. Seen from a scientific perspective, "nesting" kind of makes sense.

Chaos, Disorder, and Entropy

One of the most important laws of nature can be summed up in the statement that disorder—or entropy—increases, no matter what happens. An example is a melting ice cube. Water molecules are first neatly ordered next to each other, but as the ice melts, they break away from one another, and start twisting and shaking, becoming one big watery mess. It's easier to clean up an ice cube than a puddle of water.

Freezer

"Aha!" You might be thinking. "I'll just put the water in the freezer. It'll turn into ice, and order shall be restored—right?"

Not so fast. Yes, order will appear to be restored—but the net disorder will still increase. That's because the heat produced by a freezer's motor will have air molecules whirling around in all directions. The disorder this creates is actually greater than the disorder that disappears due to the water freezing.

Messes Get Messier

Another example is a coffee cup. When it falls, it breaks. A coffee cup will never fall and become whole. When you see shards flying toward each other to form a whole cup, you know that you're watching a film playing backward. In films running forward, things always become messier. Because objects easily fall apart, but never fall and become whole, the disorder in the world is always growing.

Order in the Disorder

Life seems to be able to mock this law of nature. Life creates temporary oases of order in the growing desert of disorder. A living organism is somehow able to temporarily stop the disorder, or even reverse it. From little pieces of lime a shell can be created; earth and air can become a tree leaf. A living being creates order in its own body—to repair fractures, build muscles, create brain synapses, and fight deterioration.

However, just as in the case of the freezer, the law of entropy dictates that a living being will still increase overall external disorder. We do this the same way the freezer does—by donating heat to the environment. In addition, our bodies feed on the "orderly material" generated by other living organisms, and discharge it as "disorder." We eat beautiful apples and discharge a disorderly mass, so the general disorder keeps growing.

If we make sure that our house stays in order, then our home becomes a kind of living organism, separate from the disordered, decaying outside world, where things only become increasingly dusty. Where things are put in place and cleared away, "life" rules. The fact that the net disorder on earth grows even faster because of all this cleaning (landfills, pollution), is another story.

More information: What Is Life? *by Erwin Schrödinger (Cambridge University Press)*

The Little One

Some experts say that an embryo officially becomes a fetus this week. (Others prefer week 10 or 11.) Semantics aside, the little guy is now somewhere around—or north of—three-quarters of an inch. The arms and legs are developing: muscles and bones are appearing, making it possible for the baby to make his first kicks (though they can't yet be felt). The tail has more or less disappeared. Hair follicles and nipples are appearing. At the end of the legs, tiny toes are visible. The baby's heartbeat may be audible now with the Doppler device. Try to join your partner if she goes to the doctor, as she will probably want to share this moment with you: a brave little heart, doing its best to beat fast.

The Big One

Often, this is a tough week for a pregnant woman. Irritability is very common, and she can also feel overwhelmed with stress and anxiety. How will everything work out? At times you may catch her staring at you with a somewhat pitying look on her face. She probably won't say it out loud, but she may be having thoughts along the lines of, "Just look at him sitting there; he has no clue what he's in for. He can't clean, he can't plan, and he always thinks that everything will work out on its own. Poor thing." If you notice that she seems more stressed out every time she looks at you, you might want to suggest taking a walk together. Stress is not good for a pregnant woman, and walking reduces tension. (See "Stress and Pregnancy," page 94.) An additional benefit is that most men find it easier to talk when they're walking. Chances are, you can surprise her during your walk with some sensitive and possibly even clever remarks that might increase her faith in you and reduce her stress.

The Little One

The baby is now about 1.5 inches long. The arms and legs are growing fast, and the arms are able to bend. The webbing between the fingers and the toes is disappearing, tooth buds are growing, and the neck and ears are developing.

The Big One

To put it mildly, you've moved down a spot in the hierarchy. To put it less mildly, whatever you're thinking, feeling, and wanting is absolutely unimportant for now. When your partner wakes up in the morning, she thinks about the baby. Same thing when she goes to bed at night. And when, over dinner, you're talking about the funny and/or profound matters that filled your day, she's probably not listening because her head is inside her belly. It's not much fun for you, but this is not the time to act miserable and discontented. Practice empathy. It may not be your strong suit—you're a man, after all—but try and do your best. Imagine having a baby inside of you, and . . . oh, right, never mind. Anyway, you will need to control yourself if you feel that you're not getting enough attention.

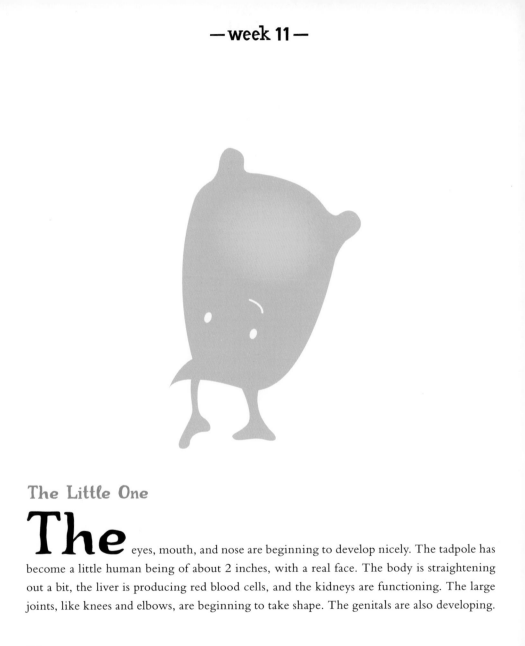

The Little One

The eyes, mouth, and nose are beginning to develop nicely. The tadpole has become a little human being of about 2 inches, with a real face. The body is straightening out a bit, the liver is producing red blood cells, and the kidneys are functioning. The large joints, like knees and elbows, are beginning to take shape. The genitals are also developing.

The Big One

Your partner may possibly start behaving a little weird. She loves food she used to hate, and the other way round. All of a sudden she'll no longer enjoy a nice cup of coffee with steamed milk. Try to keep your potential paranoia under control. Real life is not a movie, and your partner's body has not been taken over by an alien life form. It's absolutely normal that her behavior is a bit strange. It's all the fault of hormones.

The Little One

The fetus is around 2.5 inches, and weighs about a half-ounce. The eyes, which were first located on the side of the head, are getting closer to the front, and the ears are now in the right place. Little nails are starting to grow on the fingers, and the pituitary has started producing hormones.

The Big One

The baby's heartbeat is usually audible now through the doctor's Doppler. If you go along to the doctor visit, it's possible you'll be sitting there like a zombie, not knowing exactly how to react to everything being said. That's okay; it comes with the territory if you're a guy. However, this does not mean that you're not important. Listen carefully to all the explanations the doctor is giving, as your partner may not remember everything.

DNA, CHROMOSOMES, AND GENES

Naturally, every man knows what chromosomes and DNA are. That's why your kid has blue or brown eyes. That's genetics. Right? Just to be sure, here are the facts again. You don't absolutely have to read or care about this stuff, but you might find it interesting after your baby is born and you're trying to figure out how it got blue eyes from two brown-eyed parents.

We're made up of many trillions of cells (estimated at around 37 trillion): skin cells, liver cells, brain cells, etc. A cell consists of a membrane—that's the little bag that keeps everything together—and a nucleus, the cell's central HQ. The cell is filled with fluid containing dissolved salts, fats, carbohydrates, and proteins. Cells can be seen as microscopic factories where both the machines and the workers are made of protein. A human body contains many thousands of different kinds of proteins: stiff, structural proteins, as can be found in hair and in the skin, and proteins such as hemoglobin which can hold oxygen.

All proteins are made of building blocks called amino acids. Just as you can build a great variety of things—fire trucks, houses, trees, etc.—from only a few types of Legos, proteins with very diverse shapes and functions in the human body are created from just 20 types of amino acids.

Blueprint

The creation of proteins is not a random process. Proteins are built according to a strict blueprint, and this blueprint is laid down in the DNA molecule folded up inside the nucleus of each cell. A DNA molecule resembles a long, twisted rope ladder. The ropes consist of materials chemists call deoxyribose (sugar) and phosphates. The rungs connecting the ropes consist of two halves that fit together exactly. These halves are made up of four materials: thymine (T), adenine (A), cytosine (C), and guanine (G).

Forget these difficult names and imagine, just as with amino acids, building blocks that can be clicked together. Thymine and adenine fit together nicely, and cytosine and guanine do, too. But thymine does not go together with guanine, and adenine does not click on cytosine. To use another metaphor, a DNA molecule is like two totem poles with hands that cling together and hold each other. A T-hand will always hold on to an A-hand, and a C-hand will always hold on to a G-hand.

Sequence

When you separate the two totem poles, one string will be the negative of the other. Half a DNA molecule can be used as a mold to make the other half. At first sight, the sequence of the hands appears to be random, like ATGTACCGTGGATAA. But the sequence of the "letters" is less random than it seems. It's the building plan of a simple protein. The sequence shows how the amino acids should be clicked together. The code above means:

ATG: start
TAC: take amino acid tyrosine
CGT: take amino acid arginine
GGA: take amino acid glycine
TAA: stop

Such a piece of DNA code, which corresponds with the building formula of one protein, is called a gene.

String

DNA can also be compared to a CD with zeroes and ones, while the proteins are the music you hear when you're playing that CD. But DNA is not a disc; it's a string over two yards long. The genetic material in a single DNA molecule is so long, it would be a big mess if it weren't encased in a harness of proteins. The combination of a DNA molecule and the harness is called a chromosome.

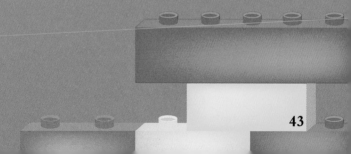

The chromosome's harness also guarantees that not all genes in a cell become active. For example, the gene for blue eyes will remain encased tightly inside a muscle cell, but it will be activated in an eye cell. The proteins roll out the relevant piece of DNA for a short while so DNA can be copied. Such a copy of one gene is called mRNA. To use another musical image: just as a player piano makes music from the holes in the paper roll, proteins called ribosomes use mRNA to build proteins.

Chromosome Pairs

Chromosomes consist of pairs. Usually, a person has 46 chromosomes, divided into 23 pairs. Each chromosome pair contains a chromosome from the father and one from the mother. There are 22 pairs of chromosomes known as autosomes, and one pair of sex chromosomes. The autosomes (any non-sex chromosome) are numbered from 1 to 22 according to decreasing length: the longest chromosome is chromosome 1 and the shortest one is chromosome 22. The sex hormones are indicated with an X or a Y. A woman has two X chromosomes; one from the father and one from the mother. A man has an XY chromosome pair, the only chromosome pair where both chromosomes do not have the same length.

Eyes

Because most chromosomes are double, the genes are double as well. Each protein has a double building plan—one originating from the father, and one from the mother. That's why a father with blood type A and a mother with type B can have children with blood type AB. The same goes for the color of the eyes, where a child can have what's known as blue-brown eyes. Blue-brown eyes look brown. That's why brown is the dominant color in this case. A father with blue-brown eyes and a mother with blue-brown eyes both have eyes that seem brown. They can have children with brown-brown, blue-brown, and blue-blue eyes. The first two will appear brown and the last one will be blue.

Colorblindness

The fact that there are two almost-identical proteins for one function is a built-in safety measure. Should there be a defect in the mother's gene, then usually the father's gene can compensate for it. But not always. The fact is, men have one chromosome pair which is not symmetrical, the XY chromosome. For a man, a defect on the X chromosome has consequences. A known example is red–green colorblindness, which for this reason appears more often in men than in women.

More information: The Annotated and Illustrated Double Helix *by James D. Watson (Simon & Schuster)*

45

the 2nd TRIMESTER!

For your partner—which means for you as well—this is the start of an energetic period. She'll be as happy as Bob the Builder. She has the energy of three people, she's bursting with ideas, she has red cheeks, and she'll paint the nursery just like that.

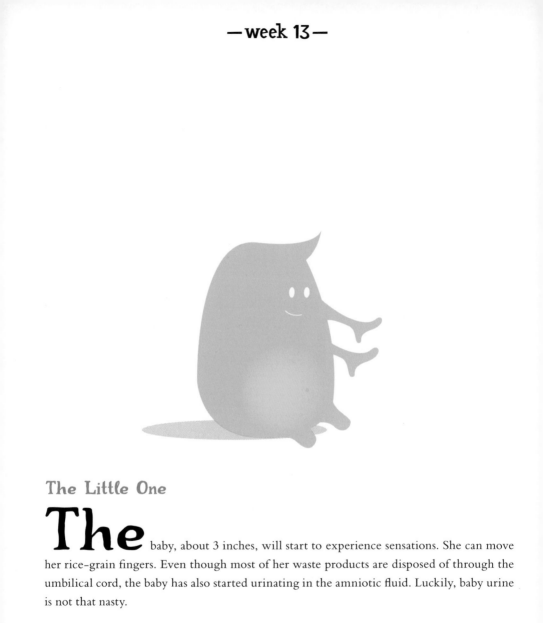

The Little One

The baby, about 3 inches, will start to experience sensations. She can move her rice-grain fingers. Even though most of her waste products are disposed of through the umbilical cord, the baby has also started urinating in the amniotic fluid. Luckily, baby urine is not that nasty.

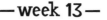

The Big One

Lots of women will wait until this week to start sharing the big news with anyone who's willing to listen. They'll have plenty to chat and scream about on the phone, and the emails will start coming in. You should realize that the way women talk to each other is different from the way men discuss matters. It's not, "Hi, I'm pregnant," and "Oh, congrats." A lot more needs to be said on the subject. And if you feel that it's a lot of empty words, you're not entirely mistaken, but it's also much more than it appears to be. The conversations are actually very precise in a manner that's incomprehensible to men. The social clocks are synchronized. How does A react; how does B react; what are my friendships like? Who won't be any good? Who reacted differently than expected? The brain sectors for emotional and social intelligence are working overtime. The exact meaning of all of this will forever remain unclear to most men. So let the women chat and just appreciate that it has its purpose.

The Little One

Now
about 3.5 inches, the baby might be starting to grow hair, as well as downy body hair called lanugo. Ovaries or the prostate gland are beginning to form. The neck is also becoming longer and more neck-like.

The Big One

If your partner is still sick and hormonal, it should diminish during this week. But don't get too excited: she'll probably have a list of chores that she wants done. A new kitchen, now. Get out of your study to turn it into a nursery, now. Tidy up the yard, or the garage, now. Emphasis on "now." There's no use fighting it. Best thing is to just help out. Now. And in the meantime, try to see if she's eating enough, and eating healthy. If the pots are empty and she's staring at your plate looking hungry, give her some of your food. Let her stay in her happy pregnancy bubble. Bring her home some feel-good magazines, buy some bath salts, run a bath for her and let her soak in the warm water. If you like watching the news at night, make sure that it doesn't bother her. She may not want to see misery or political backstabbing, but might enjoy *Downton Abbey* or a nice movie on DVD. Make sure that one day she'll be able to look back on her pregnancy as a great, positive experience, and not a period of Mideast conflict, when the stock market collapsed and the New England Patriots didn't win the Super Bowl.

The Little One

The baby, around 4.5 inches now, is starting to move around, kick, suck his thumb, and wiggle his digits. The kidneys continue their development (and baby starts "breathing" amniotic fluid, which is largely urine), while bones continue to develop.

The Big One

If you're having a night out, to be completely safe, your partner shouldn't drink alcohol. And keep in mind, even though you may believe you're at your funniest after a six-pack of beer, she probably won't agree. She's already changed, as you may have noticed. But that's not entirely fair. To fully understand her, try going to a party and not drinking. You'll probably wonder, along with your pregnant partner, why people are making corny jokes and behaving so childishly. That's what a party looks like when you're not drinking. Thank goodness you have a good reason to go home early.

The Little One

The eyebrows have appeared and the baby (between 4 and 5 inches) is getting a real face, which she can use, as if she understands, to make faces. The baby can move her eyes and see light.

strawberry

egg

cheese

licorice

←salami

lettuce

chocolate sauce

The Big One

We have good news and bad news. Around this time, a pregnant woman encounters an entirely new feeling inside her belly. It feels like a little bit of gas, but different. She feels the baby floundering and tumbling. This is the good news. The bad news is that more and more little aches and pains start to pop up: backaches, dizziness, swollen ankles and hands. This is a good time to bring home some hot-water bottles and heat packs.

You should not be surprised when your partner stumbles down the stairs in the middle of the night to raid the pantry for beef jerky, lard, or pickles. Don't worry too much that these food attacks might be bad for the baby. A weird snack every now and then won't do much harm.

This week, your partner may want to make an appointment for the 20-week screening ultrasound. (See also page 16.)

STAR-DUST

"We are stardust." This is not only a truly beautiful line for a birth announcement, it's also true.

Birth announcements are not really a guy thing. It's hard to make profound statements about childbirth without using clichés. Just look at all the announcement cards: *Our little miracle has arrived*, or *The moon or the sun? You are both.* But there's likely no way you can get out of helping to think about the text on the birth announcement. In fact, your partner is probably hoping somewhere deep down that you will make a sensitive, spiritual contribution. You may be thinking of a quote along the lines of, "That's it, now let's get back to my normal life," or "There goes my dream of being a rock star." Funny, sure, but many women do not have a sense of humor when it comes to birth announcements.

Salvation

Thank goodness, there is salvation. With a little knowledge of astronomy you can come up with a beautiful, honest, sincere sentiment which will do justice to the occasion, will not be overly sappy or cute, and which even pregnant women will like. Something like:

"Every little nail, every little hair, every little eyelash . . . is made of stardust."

Stardust? Yes, stardust. Everything you see around you, everything you touch or break, is made of stardust. Everything on earth is made of one of the over ninety elements that appear in nature. Elements are the basic ingredients of everything you see around you. For example, hydrogen, oxygen, nitrogen, iron, and gold. And most of them are created in a star that was at least eight times larger than our sun. A bright ball of fire which disappeared with a big bang hundreds of millions of years ago.

In the Beginning . . .

Right after the Big Bang, the universe was pitch black and filled with dark clouds of hydrogen. Hydrogen is the simplest element in existence, consisting of a proton with a positive charge, linked to an electron with a negative charge. You may imagine a hydrogen atom as a proton surrounded by an electron turning in circles. It is considered number 1 of the elements.

The hydrogen clouds slowly became compact and spherical due to gravity. After a while, the pressure in the center of such spheres was so enormous that the hydrogen atoms were fused into helium atoms, a process we call nuclear fusion. A helium atom is the second-simplest element. You may consider a helium atom as the product of two hydrogen atoms; the number 2 of the elements.★

★*In fact, four hydrogen atoms make one helium atom. But if you want to know why, you'll have to go deeper into the matter.*

Nuclear fusion is as if you're squeezing two marbles together so hard that they turn into one marble. The funny thing is, this one marble is lighter than the two original marbles. When you compress hydrogen atoms into helium atoms, mass is lost. The mass that disappears is turned into energy, according to Einstein's famous law:

$$E = mc^2$$

Here, E is energy, m is mass (grams), and c is the speed of light (300,000,000 meters per second). The speed of light squared (c^2), is a very large number. So you only need a little bit of mass to produce a lot of energy. The energy, resulting from compressing hydrogen into helium, disappears as electromagnetic waves; light and gamma radiation. After the Big Bang, there was a moment that a hydrogen cloud, due to its own gravity, was compressed so much that this process was initiated, and started to generate light. And then, one by one, other little lights started to appear in the universe.

Heavy and in Their Element

So, a star can be seen as a spherical cloud of hydrogen, where the outer layers press on the inner layers. This causes the pressure in the center to be so intense that a continuously exploding H-bomb in the center of that cloud pushes the hydrogen outside again. The result is a light-emitting spherical balance, a star or sun. If the hydrogen in the center of the star is gone, a new nuclear fusion process will start with helium atoms fusing into even heavier elements. This continues up to the element iron (number 26). Iron is the heaviest element created by nuclear fusion. Heavier elements, such as gold (79), and lead (82), cannot be created by nuclear fusion.

Supernova

When iron is created in the deepest interior of a star, something serious occurs. The large star motor begins to stutter. The outward pressure disappears and the gas ball collapses due to the gravity. Additionally, so much energy is released—due to friction and quantum-mechanical and gravity processes—that the star explodes. If the star is more than eight times heavier than our sun, the elements gold and lead will be created in such a supernova explosion. The only thing remaining is a dark cloud of dust and gas, containing the more than ninety elements known to us on earth.

Our solar system was created from such a cloud. When you look at your hands, you will see little biological structures, constructed out of the material that is made inside a gigantic star. Our sun is nothing compared to that star. So you can say, with a straight face:

"Made of stardust. Created in the heart of a star."

That's a great line for a birth announcement card.

And it's also very poetic to tell a mom-to-be:

"And the ring I have in my pocket is made of materials that were created when a star exploded in an enormous explosion of cosmic passion."

And it is—that is, if you really have a silver or gold ring in your pocket when you're saying it.

More information: Stardust *by John Gribbin with Mary Gribbin (Yale University Press)*

The Little One

The baby (around 5 inches) is putting on fat, which will be important after birth for both heat and energy. Some women will notice that laughter or sneezing are sometimes answered by a little kick in the stomach. That's the baby reacting to her antics. If your partner doesn't feel anything yet, this doesn't necessarily mean anything. Sometimes it'll take a few more weeks.

The Big One

Your partner looks very healthy. She has a rosy complexion. Her organs are receiving extra blood. Yes, all her organs. If you're lucky, maybe you'll get lucky.

The Little One

The baby is growing fast now and is already nearly 5.5 inches and 5 to 7 ounces. The body continues to catch up with the large head, and proportions are becoming better balanced. The baby's fingerprints are also forming now.

The Big One

Look

at her belly button. If it hasn't popped out yet, it could happen any moment now. Maybe you'll be one of those very few men who see their partner's belly button pop out. During this phase of the pregnancy, your partner may suffer from dizziness and shortness of breath. And she may develop dark spots on her skin. If she's pregnant during the summer, she may want to use sunscreen with a high SPF to prevent pigmentation spots. A pigment mustache may not make her feel very beautiful.

Pop

The Little One

The proportions of the fetus (about 6 inches) now resemble those of a full-grown baby. The baby is also moving quite a bit now, even doing somersaults, though your partner may not yet feel them.

The Big One

Your

partner may start having stabbing abdominal pains caused by the stretching of the womb and surrounding ligaments and muscles. Very unpleasant, but normal. Please note: if she's having nasty, stabbing pains, it may be annoying if you start telling her in a doctor's voice that this is normal.

The Little One

The baby is now about 6.5 inches long. This is an important time for the skin, which now consists of two layers: the dermis and the epidermis. The baby seems to be covered in a fatty ointment that protects the skin, called vernix caseosa. If the baby is a girl, she will now have a uterus and ovaries (with developing eggs).

The Big One

Around

this time, the second-trimester ultrasound is performed. Make sure that you'll be present, because it's very special to see your baby do flips. For many men this is the moment they realize for the first time that this is not all a big joke; something is definitely there inside that belly. It's also nice to be together in case of anything unexpected or unclear; you'll both be able to hear what the doctor or technician has to say, and compare notes afterward.

69

BOY OR GIRL?

Around week 18, an ultrasound can show whether you're having a boy or a girl. But the gender was already decided during conception. You, as the man, determine the baby's gender.

Whether it's a boy or a girl depends on your sperm. The egg will always contain an X chromosome, but the sperm contains either an X or Y chromosome. If the fertilized egg is XX, it will become a girl. If it's XY, it will become a boy. During the first couple months after conception there's no difference between the development of a boy or girl. After that, testicles develop in a male embryo, under the influence of the XY chromosome pair. The testicles start producing testosterone, the penis starts to grow, and eventually the testicles drop.

Hormonal Swings

Testosterone is responsible for all essential differences between boys and girls.

The testosterone level in a pregnant woman's body is not only determined by hormones produced by a male fetus; stress and smoking can also influence her testosterone. Additionally, not every fetus is exposed to the same amount of testosterone in the womb. That's why there are tomboys and girly-girls. The more testosterone in utero, the more boyish the girl will be. Of course, there are almost no girls without boyish characteristics or boys without girlish characteristics.

Boy and Girl Brains

In newborns, the only striking difference between girls and boys seem to be their genitals. But since conception, their brains have been developing differently. A boy's brain is larger and heavier than a girl's brain. The connections between the two hemispheres also develop differently due to testosterone. This difference can be noticed fairly soon after the birth: boy babies tend to be more interested in objects (such as a mobile over the crib), and girl babies are more interested in faces.

Bath of Testosterone

Chances are you're a bit uncomfortable with all the emotions surrounding pregnancy and childbirth. That's nothing to be ashamed of. After all, it's not your fault that, as a fetus, you were hanging out in a bath of testosterone for months, is it? But in the coming months you'll probably also discover some of your own unexpected feminine aspects. The testosterone level in that bath was not always that high, and your brain has its feminine facets as well.

More information: Sex and Cognition *by Doreen Kimura (Bradford Books);* Brain Gender *by Melissa Hines (Oxford University Press);* The Female Brain *by Louann Brizendine (Harmony).*

The Little One

The
baby (7 inches and 11 ounces, give or take) is now drinking the amniotic fluid, and his intestines will process it, creating stool called meconium. If everything is in order, the baby will only pass the meconium after birth. You have no idea what you're in for. But you'll find that out later.

The Big One

It's
always a good idea to pick out a nice movie for a pleasant evening at home. But take a good look at the ratings. Don't choose anything violent or extremely scary. Your best bet is to go with movies rated G. Even then, don't be surprised if she ends up crying for half the movie. You should also be prepared for possible nasty remarks. You don't have to do much to annoy her, there's not a lot she can do about it. Her body has been taken over by hormones. Try to take it with a sense of humor, so at least you'll get to laugh about it. On the other hand, some women become surprisingly even-keeled and pleasant during pregnancy. If that's the case, enjoy it.

The Little One

The fetus is now a real mini-baby—exactly like a real baby, with little pink lips, eyebrows, and lashes—but only about 8 inches long. The bones are beginning to harden and, if you're having a boy, the testicles are beginning to drop.

The Big One

The baby's kicks are getting more noticeable, and it's clear that the baby couldn't care less about anything or anyone. He will start kicking just when you want to go to sleep, and he will sleep quietly when you would like a sign of life. The baby does his own thing. Better get used to it.

The Little One

The baby is now 8 or so inches. She continues to practice her breathing, and sometimes grabs the umbilical cord with her little hands. Her skin is red, and looks a bit like the skin of a large raisin. It's loose to provide extra room for the fat that will be stored in the coming weeks.

The Big One

Your
partner may be secretly worrying about the baby's growth, but she probably doesn't need to. If she's not consuming sufficient nutrients, the baby is smart enough to simply get them from her mother's body. For example, if she's not getting enough calcium, the baby will just take it out of her bones. So try to see that she's drinking milk every once in a while, or make her a cheese sandwich. When you're grocery shopping, you should stock up on dairy products such as yogurt and anything containing calcium and vitamin D.

The Little One

The
baby is now around 8.5 inches and weighs 1.5 pounds. He's developed a sleep-wake cycle. He may also have a decent amount of hair. In addition, his inner ear is developed, which means he'll start getting a sense of balance—and an entirely different feel for his environment.

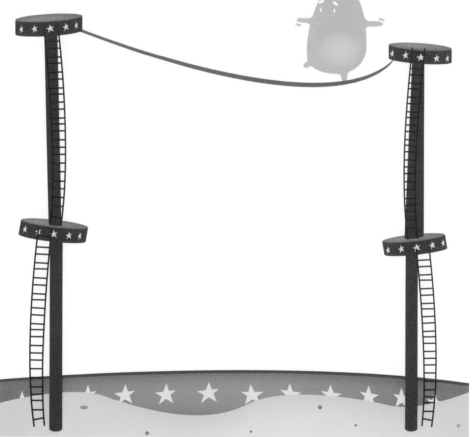

The Big One

This may be a good time to stop and think about sleep. People who worry a lot don't sleep well. And people who don't sleep well will worry a lot. It's a chicken-and-egg problem where most people look at the chicken (worry), but they should also keep an eye on the egg (sleep). So make sure you get enough sleep. Even more importantly, make sure that she gets enough sleep. If she really likes a cup of coffee after dinner, secretly give her decaf. Turn off the TV a bit earlier at night. Make sure the bedroom is clean and organized, and get some fresh flowers. More than any other organ, the nose keeps working at full power during sleep, so it's really true that you'll have better dreams when it smells nice. And pleasant dreams are invaluable for a pregnant woman. Just imagine what kind of nightmares you would have if there were a parasitic creature living inside you.

BRAIN

DEVELOPMENT

In addition to genetic factors, environmental factors are important to the brain's development. To ensure that the baby's brain develops properly, it's very important now that your partner eats well and is as happy as possible.

Brain Cell Factory

It is paradoxical that a brain could develop to the point where it could ask how it came into existence. Nevertheless, this is what happens—and some brains are so developed, they actually have a pretty good idea how they got that way. In the young embryo, about two weeks after fertilization, three cell layers are created: the ectoderm, endoderm, and mesoderm (see Week 5, page 20). The ectoderm, besides giving rise to the skin, hair, and nails, is also the foundation for the brain and nervous system. The process starts when a layer of cells called the neural plate forms within the ectoderm. In the middle of the neural plate, a groove appears, and the edges of the plate curl and bend toward one another. Gradually, this plate rolls into a tube. The neural tube is kind of a sushi roll inside the embryo, and it develops to become the nervous system and brain.

Folic Acid

Normally, both ends of the tube eventually close up around week 6. If the tube does not close properly, it could lead to spina bifida or anencephaly. Both genetic and environmental factors appear to contribute to these conditions; taking folic acid will reduce the risk of neural-tube defects. In a normally developing neural tube, three primary brain vesicles form, which eventually become the brain and spinal cord.

Brain Cell Factory

The inside of the neural tube now emerges as a brain cell factory, creating thousands of new neurons per minute through the division of nerve cells. Gradually, a layer of dividing nerve cells forms around the developing brain cavities on the inside of the tube. Nerve cells migrate to form the cerebral cortex, the brain's outer layer.

The cerebral cortex will ultimately consist of six layers. If the cell migration process doesn't go properly—for example, if neurons don't migrate far enough—it's called a cell migration disorder, and the results can be life-threatening. Although such disorders can have genetic origins, they can also be caused by the mother's use of alcohol, drugs, and certain medications during pregnancy.

Branches

After the nerve cells have reached their final positions, they will begin to grow branches that will lengthen to form connections with other neurons. These connections are called synapses, and the branches can be thought of as power lines connecting cells. The development of synapses begins halfway through the second trimester, and continues throughout one's life. There are two types: dendrites, which receive signals, and axons, which send signals. The development of these connections is not only controlled by genes; environmental factors, such as the mother's health, nutrition, and mental state, also contribute. (See Stress and Pregnancy, page 94.) If you want your baby's brain to develop well, take good care of your partner.

Myelin

Finally, a layer of myelin develops around the axons. Myelin is a kind of grease that helps electrical signals fire more quickly. Myelin appears shortly after birth near the neurons that are responsible for the senses of touch, smell, and hearing, and eventually around the neurons regulating the more complex associative and cognitive functions. Finally, the cerebral hemispheres of the prefrontal cortex (which governs, among other things, planning and understanding of consequences) are myelinated, a process that will continue into adolescence. With many men, it seems as if this process has not been properly completed. With a more fully developed prefrontal cortex, you might not have needed this little book.

The Little One

He is now 9 inches tall, and somewhere between 1.5 and 2 pounds. The baby already has thoughts and memories. He can now recognize not only his mother's voice, but also yours. He's probably thinking something along the lines of, "Hey, I've heard that macho voice before."

The Big One

Some women have a problem with the extra weight they're gaining. They'll start worrying about the shape of their belly and the rest of their body. Try to understand that she wants to have a beautiful pregnancy. Don't make any jokes referring to rhinos, hippos, manatees, or humpback whales. Not even when she does so herself.

The Little One

The baby is now at least 9 inches long and weighs around 2 pounds, or just under. The baby may start to open her eyes a bit, but can only see light and darkness. You can try shining a flashlight on your partner's belly and saying something in Morse code.

The Big One

What you can do right now is ask yourself (that means not out loud) what hippos and whales enjoy, and extrapolate that to your partner. The answer, primarily, is lying comfortably submerged in water. In water, you're weightless. So if you have a bathtub, run it with warm water and fragrant bath salts. Oftentimes, pregnant women suffer from backaches. And a hot bath is great for that, too.

The Little One

The baby, at around 2 pounds and about 9.5 inches long, is starting to build up an immune system with the help of antibodies delivered through the placenta. And even though she still has some time left, the baby's lungs are continuing to develop steadily.

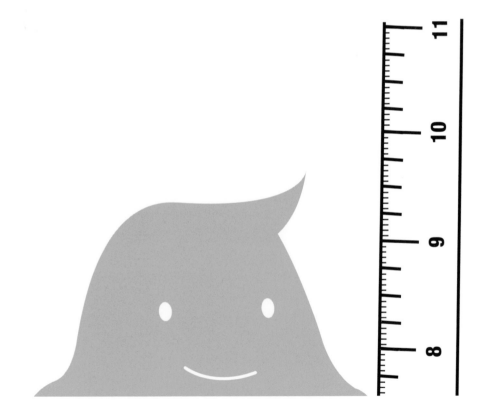

The Big One

You may have noticed, pregnant women are scatterbrained. They forget all kind of things, and sometimes processing complicated information seems impossible. This is often called "pregnancy fog" or "pregnancy brain." One of the reasons is the aforementioned fact that pregnant women often don't sleep very well. Another is the fact that baby's brain growth takes place at the expense of the mother's brain. Because the baby needs a lot of fatty acids, it's thought that the fatty acid level of the pregnant woman's blood will diminish, causing fewer fatty acids to reach the mother's brain. In fact, pregnant women's brains shrink a bit. Get used to it. Sure, experts say that the brain will be restored (or even better than new) after birth, but with the sleep deprivation and hormonal changes of new motherhood, things can stay foggy a long time.

the
3rd

WORLD
CHAMP

TRIMESTER!

Now it's really going to happen. The baby is kicking. He can hear and feel you. And you can hear, see, and feel him. Slowly but surely you can start getting ready for the launch.

The Little One

This is an important week. If born now, the baby has a ninety percent chance of survival. The baby is about 10 inches from head to rump (and 16 inches from head to toe), and weighs around 2.5 pounds. In the coming weeks, the baby's weight could triple. The baby can open his eyes a little more now and even experience REM sleep.

At some point you will most likely hear your partner complain about having a tight belly. This is probably due to contractions of the uterine muscles, known as Braxton-Hicks contractions. These may help the uterus prepare for labor. During these practice contractions, the belly becomes hard and tight. It's not exactly painful, but it's uncomfortable. The baby still has more than enough room to move around, and it absolutely will not hurt him.

The Big One

If you once believed that pretty girls poop glass marbles and never fart or burp, you've probably learned a lot by now. Pregnant women often experience problems with digestion. For starters, pregnancy hormones loosen the closure between the esophagus and stomach, so stomach acid can easily come up. A fried steak with hot sauce and a Coke is not the type of food you should give a pregnant woman. Dairy products, nuts, cereal, and potatoes are much better choices.

STRESS
AND PREGNANCY

Are the two of you feeling a little stressed? There's nothing wrong with that. Not even when you're pregnant. But your partner shouldn't be stressed too long. It's not great for her or the baby.

When you're stressed, your body produces cortisol, which helps keep you alert. However, in pregnant women, cortisol isn't such a good thing. For one thing, cortisol is associated with preterm birth. Maternal stress has also been associated with low birth weight. Research has shown that children with a lower birth weight will more often develop cardiovascular diseases and diabetes as adults.

Besides this, cortisol can also reach the fetus's bloodstream through the placenta. And that's probably not good for the baby. Research has indicated that the cell division of the hippocampus in rat fetuses progressed more slowly when cortisol from the mother was passed to the placenta, resulting in fewer brain cells being produced.

Lowered IQ

There are also indications that the children of women who were stressed during pregnancy have lower IQs than those whose mothers were not stressed. Additionally, some researchers link emotional, behavioral, and sleep problems in children whose moms were stressed while pregnant.

Miracles

Clearly, stress should be avoided—and one of the main causes of stress for a pregnant woman is relationship problems. If there's one thing you can do to make yourself useful right now, it's ensuring that you two are having a good time together. In practice, this means that you should pay attention when your partner is talking to you. And if you're not keeping up, then make sure you look at her every now and then, and nod and growl in approval.

To make a pregnant woman even happier, a good housecleaning will work miracles. Or help out getting the nursery ready. If she says something along the lines of, "And the nursery is also far from finished," you should run to Home Depot and get a couple buckets of bright water-based paint. Also make sure that you spend a lot of time at home. Leave work early, skip a game night, and perhaps this year take a pass on camping with the guys. It's better for your boss and your buddies to be disappointed than your partner. It's that simple. Put on your slippers, turn on a CD with bird sounds, and light a scented candle. In Japan they practice something called *taikyo* in connection with pregnancy, and it involves thinking happy thoughts, singing songs, touching the belly, and talking to the unborn baby. And maybe that's not as silly as it seems.

The Little One

The baby is about ready. The organs have taken shape. The baby is "breathing" in utero. Now, mostly what's left is building brain cells, developing the lungs, and putting on weight. A lot.

The Big One

A pregnant woman sweats a lot and urinates often, and should therefore drink a lot. Make sure there's always a drink ready for her—and we're not talking cups and glasses, but jugs and bottles. Don't give her a mug of tea but an entire pot, or make her a fresh smoothie. Throw some juice, bananas, and yogurt in a blender and let it whirl. If you don't own a blender, this is the perfect time to bring one home and use it proudly.

The Little One

The baby (10.5 inches or so, and around 3 pounds) is now growing more slowly in length, but all the more quickly in weight. In addition, she's already producing hormones that will help to ensure that her mother's milk production gets going.

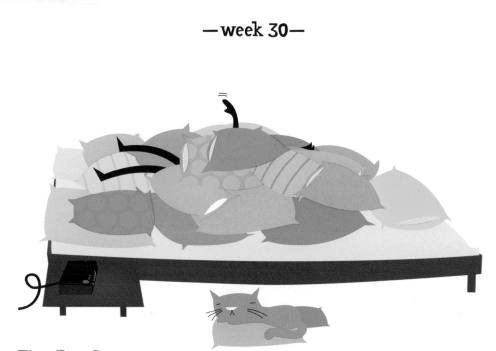

The Big One

It's becoming increasingly difficult to get a good night's sleep as she nears the end of her pregnancy. She has to pee constantly, and with her heavy belly it's more and more difficult to find a comfortable sleeping position (and even to get out of bed). Conventional wisdom holds that it's best for pregnant women to sleep on their left side, which is said to enable optimal blood flow and take some pressure off the liver. She'll also be more comfortable with a few pillows around her, behind her, and between her legs. A body pillow or long pregnancy pillow is perfect, and she may be able to use it later for nursing and sleeping as well. You will also make a pregnant woman very happy with a microwavable pad or pillow, preferably filled with something natural like lavender, rice, cherry pits, or buckwheat hulls. Such pillows are also great in the final stages of the pregnancy, when she has to handle contractions. But we'll get to that later.

The Little One

The

baby is somewhere between 10.5 and 11 inches crown to rump, and around 3.5 pounds. He has a nice, round belly. The bone marrow is busy producing red blood cells, and his brain is growing at quite a clip. The baby may also be making little rhythmic bumps. That's when he has the hiccups.

The Big One

If your partner asks you to do an unpleasant chore such as cleaning the gutters, touching up the chipped baseboards in the hall, or removing cobwebs from the ceilings, you should look alive. Put down your newspaper, cancel band practice, and turn off your cell phone. At the very least, make sure that you get to it fairly promptly. Not that you should wait on her hand and foot (unless she's on bed rest, in which case you should probably be her slave), but a pregnant woman is determined when it comes to household chores deemed urgent. If you won't do them, she'll do them herself—and she'll get on a stool on top of a chair on top of a table if need be, without hesitation, to remove a stain from the ceiling. The urge is just too strong.

The Little One

The baby is now about 11 inches crown to rump (or 18-odd inches head to toe), and weighs 3.75 pounds. A baby inside the belly at this point behaves much like a baby outside the belly. She's grabbing around and making funny faces, and she's an old pro now at sucking her thumb. She's also a pro now at REM sleep, and has started dreaming.

The Big One

As mentioned before, pregnancy hormones not only do things to the body, but also to the mind. If you've ever wondered why the world seems to need so many stores with scented candles, herbal lotions, cutting boards for bread, and fancy pillows, the answer is: progesterone. Pregnant women will buy anything, especially if it smells good. Some stores are absolute pregnantopias, full of sweet fragrances, cheerful colors, natural materials, and environmentally friendly baby toys. But a pregnant woman's spending spree also has a positive side. The fact that you're reading this little book is one of them. Because let's be honest—you didn't buy this book yourself.

The Little One

The baby is about 19 inches head to toe, and around 4.5 pounds. The downy hair that covered his body to keep it warm is disappearing.

The Big One

Your

partner is interested in matters you're simply not ready for. You haven't even considered them for a second. A good example is the stroller, which is a kind of multifunctional amphibious vehicle you can put your baby in. You can get a very good baby stroller for a good price, but that might not do you any good. It's kind of like cars: lots of men want to drive nice, expensive cars to show that they're doing all right. In the same way, lots of new mothers like to push a Bugaboo around. It shows what kind of mother she is, and makes it easier to meet other mothers with high-profile strollers. It turns out that this is almost an exact science, and you probably need to be a woman to fully understand it. And where most men at some point learn to let go of their dreams and eventually drive a Toyota, women are unyielding. For many women a nice stroller is worth a lot. If you make enough money to get a Bugaboo or something similar, you should secretly start to save up. As long as you can afford it, and you realize that it's not at all important for the baby, it doesn't really matter. Fortunately, the really important things for the baby are free: peace, love, and breast milk.

THE CHICKEN AND THE EGG

People do not just appear. They develop bit by bit, from a fertilized egg. How does this cell division work?

Which came first, the chicken or the egg? Is there a fully formed but very tiny chicken inside the egg, and does that tiny chicken simply grow steadily in size? Or do the contents of the egg slowly turn into a chicken, step by step? The first man who seriously considered this question was Aristotle. He checked chicken eggs in different stages of development and saw how the egg whites and yolks turned into odd structures which in turn developed into the tadpole-like early stages of a chick—and then finally into a real little chick. As he discovered, there was no tiny chicken that appeared out of nothing; rather, a chicken was the creation of vague structures that underwent a slow metamorphosis.

Cellular Division

Multicellular organisms, such as humans, do not just appear all of a sudden. They develop step by step from a fertilized egg, called a zygote. The zygote divides in two, then does it again, and again, and again. During cell division, the nucleus containing the genetic material first divides in two, followed by the rest of the cell. After one cell division, the two daughter cells contain the same genetic information as the mother cell, and can each develop into a complete baby. This would produce identical twins. This hardly ever happens after two cell divisions, which is why identical quadruplets are extremely rare.

In the first few days after fertilization, a sphere of cells develops called the morula. A few days after that, a cavity develops inside the sphere, which becomes known as a blastocyst. At this point, the cells can be roughly divided into two types: cells which will become the baby (aka embryonic stem cells), and cells which will become the placenta, the organ that serves as a station between mother's and baby's circulatory systems. The split is irreversible. From an embryonic stem cell, any imaginable human cell can develop (muscles, brains, bones, etc.).

In the early nineteenth century, the embryologist Heinz Christian Pander discovered that three cell types first develop in the embryo, and they're arranged in three layers: the ectoderm, endoderm, and mesoderm. The cells in the ectoderm develop to become external organs including the skin, mouth, and nose, as well as the anus and the fingernails. The cells in the endoderm become the digestive tract and the lungs, while cells in the mesoderm become the muscles, bones, and heart tissue. Since the nineteenth century, scientists have developed increasingly improved techniques for studying groups of cells, and even individual cells, as they develop. The most important discovery is that cells do not maintain the same shape as they develop, and do not stay in the same place; some cells migrate through the embryo.

Higher Powers

For dozens of years, biologists have been asking themselves how it's possible that every cell reaches its correct position and develops the correct function. How does a cell in the eye know to become a lens, and how does a cell behind it know to become a nerve? How do cells know where they should be in the body, and where they are in relation to each other? And how do cells know when to stop dividing, because the organ they belong to is large enough? These questions seem almost impossible to answer without appealing to "higher powers." Still, biologists are increasingly able to give answers relating to the characteristics of different cells. Cells with a rougher surface will move differently than smoother cells. Also, cells influence one another with so-called signaling molecules. Some cells discharge material that moves through the organism; the closer you get to such cells, the more of this material passes by. In this way, a cell can "feel" where it is in relation to these cells.

The Little One

The baby may be as tall as 20 inches now, and probably weighs somewhere around 5 pounds. The skin is now sensitive to temperature. If you put your warm hand on the belly, the baby may snuggle against it. If the baby is a boy, his testicles are descending into his scrotum.

The Big One

You can make many pregnant women very happy with magazines about home décor, with titles such as *Better Homes and Gardens*, *Elle Décor*, and *HGTV Magazine*. These magazines are filled with spacious homes where white designer chairs consort with enormous lounge sofas. On the floor there's a sheepskin rug, and big windows offer a view to the large yard. In these pictures you'll often see a satisfied-looking woman who explains how she bought this old farmhouse for next to nothing and had it redone according to her own brilliant design. Many pregnant women love these stories, probably because it feeds the dream that a big house is achievable for smart, enterprising women who aren't afraid to do some of the work themselves. And maybe they're right. Pregnant women really do know how to get things done, and they can repaint an entire house just like that. Which is precisely the reason why, perhaps, you should not give them decorating magazines.

The Little One

The baby is still completely covered in a slippery white layer of vernix caseosa, which is thickening now (and will eventually be shed at the very end of the pregnancy). She's also gaining about half a pound every week now, and will continue to do so until labor day.

The Big One

Your partner's breasts may begin producing a watery liquid called co-lostrum. This is the preliminary stage of breast milk production. In a few weeks the baby will be full-grown, so it's good to go over the details of labor and birth with your doctor or midwife. For example, if your partner should lose her mucus plug and start spotting in week 35, that's a reason to call the doc; but in week 40, it can be a positive sign that a healthy labor is beginning. Try to imagine the delivery (see also page 132). Prepare yourself just as you would prepare for a long road trip.

113

The Little One

The baby may well be maneuvering into a good starting position for birth. It's probably getting less and less comfortable in there, as he has less and less room. If you want to, you can try influencing the baby's taste preferences. If, for example, your partner eats a lot of garlic, your baby might like it too, later on.

The Big One

Your partner's womb is pressing on her bladder. More and more strange aches and pains are appearing or getting worse, such as ligament pains and Braxton-Hicks contractions. In every pregnancy there's a moment of panic, with scared eyes and worried texts like, "OK, this pain is not OK." If the scared look lasts more than a few seconds, this is a good moment to change from Guy-Who-Doesn't-Call-the-Doctor-for-Every-Little-Thing to Man-Who-Can-Reach-the-Doctor-Really-Fast. Don't say, "Let's wait and see." Just get the phone, whether it's nighttime or the weekend. There's nothing to be afraid of. Good doctors and midwives are very patient and understanding when it comes to anything having to do with babies. And it's great for your partner if you make the phone call, and can reassure her with the doctor on the phone. If the doctor suggests waiting and seeing, and your partner still feels that something isn't right, just call again or put her in the car and take her for a ride to the emergency room. If it doesn't help, it won't hurt, either. And nobody will laugh at you in your face. At the end of the pregnancy, a pregnant woman should feel the baby moving every day. If she's not sure, get the phone. Seriously.

The hospital bag

As you pack, remember that it's okay to bring as many bags as you need. Unlike an airline, they're not going to charge you a per-bag fee.

The hospital bag(s) should contain:

- Newborn hat
- Newborn onesie
- Baby mittens to prevent scratching
- Clothes for the baby to wear home
- Pajamas for both parents
- At least one set of clothes for both parents (including underwear and socks)
- Bathing trunks (for you) if she is planning to use a labor tub
- Breastfeeding bra
- Postpartum support belt, if she plans on using one
- Toiletries for both of you, including shaving stuff

- Snacks and drinks for labor and post-partum (coconut water is great for hydration/refueling)
- At least one decent sleeping pillow for each of you
- Breastfeeding pillow
- Music players/devices/laptop
- Phone/device chargers
- Camera
- Thank-you cards for nurses
- All necessary paperwork/insurance stuff/ID cards
- Important phone numbers you may not have stored in your cell phone

It's a good idea to start packing a bag when you're not all nervous and leaving for the hospital. Take some time and do it right, at least two weeks before the due date. Even if you're planning a home birth, you should pack a hospital bag just in case. Needless to say, in an emergency situation, you're not going to be able to pack a bag in any sensible way.

Don't forget the car seat, or it will be very difficult to take the baby home. (On the other hand, if you do forget it, don't freak out. You can always go back for it, or send a relative or friend to grab it—or anything else—after the baby comes.)

PREGNANTISH-ENGLISH
DICTIONARY

When women are pregnant, they start talking on the phone a lot and using funny words. Pregnantish sounds something like this: "Let's nurse the snipped perineum, because the cervix has stripped colostrum and touched the premature. I had an immediate milk ejection reflex. Completely torn."

- *Apgar score:* The points a baby scores immediately after birth and about five minutes later for color, heart rate, reflexes, muscle tone, and breathing. (Apgar stands for appearance, pulse, grimace, activity, and respiration.)

- *Car seat:* The seat that the baby uses to ride in the car. You'll need to have one in your car before you can take the baby home from the hospital.

- *Cervix:* The lower, narrow portion of the uterus.

- *Colostrum:* The first fluid breasts produce after delivery, and sometimes before. This liquid contains many antibodies and is highly nutritious.

- *Epidural:* Anesthesia delivered into the spine through a small catheter (inserted via a needle) that stays in place during labor. Sometimes women with epidurals may control the amount of anesthetic they receive (unlike a spinal block, which completely numbs the lower body).

- *Episiotomy:* During labor, sometimes the doctor will perform a snip with scissors to make the delivery a bit easier. Let's move on, shall we?

117

- **Folic acid:** Also called vitamin B9, it's crucial for cellular division, and reduces the risk of spinal or cerebral defects.

- **Fontanel:** The soft space between the bones of the skull of an infant.

- **Induction:** To cause or strengthen contractions, often through intravenous drugs such as Pitocin.

- **Let-down (or milk ejection) reflex:** When a mother's breast milk is squeezed from the glands where it is produced (alveoli) to the mammary ducts. Sometimes a lactating woman will feel her milk let down and even leak from her breasts when she hears a baby cry or thinks about her baby.

- **Listeriosis:** Infection caused by eating unpasteurized dairy products, raw meat, unwashed produce, etc.

- **Meconium:** The baby's first bowel movement, which looks like greenish tar. Very tough and difficult to remove.

- **Membrane stripping:** A method used to encourage labor to start or to speed up. The doctor loosens the membrane of the amniotic sac from the cervix.

- **Nursing:** As in, nursing the baby. This is a less biologically descriptive term for breastfeeding, and is handy when talking to people you don't want to say "breast" to, like your boss or your mother.

- **Onesie:** A romper with short or long sleeves (note the closure at the crotch: without snaps they're useless). Onesies are theoretically very handy for diaper changing, unless there's poop leaking from the diaper (which will happen often), in which case the onesie is dirty too, and will have to be removed awkwardly (and messily) over the baby's head.

- **Oxytocin:** Hormone that stimulates contractions and is also produced during breastfeeding. Note that it sounds sort of like "Oxycontin." Perhaps not coincidentally, oxytocin sometimes induces a happy, mellow feeling in the nursing mother.

- *Pelvic floor muscles:* Imagine you have a really bad case of diarrhea, but you're trying really hard not to get your new boxers dirty. The muscles you use to accomplish this are your pelvic floor muscles.

- *Perineum:* The area between the vagina and anus.

- *Placenta:* The organ that supplies the baby with oxygen and nourishment in the womb, also known as the afterbirth.

- *Pregnant brain:* Also known as pregnancy dementia, mommy brain, etc. The confused state which begins with pregnancy and may continue well after delivery.

- *Tearing:* Usually during labor a woman will push so hard, something tears. Enough said.

- *Torn:* When you tear badly, you're torn.

- *Tummy tub:* A baby bath created in the Netherlands, shaped like a bucket, made of strong plastic.

- *Uterus:* Womb.

- *Vacuum extraction:* When the baby needs help being guided out of the birth canal, the doctor may place a suction cup on the baby's head and gently pull him out.

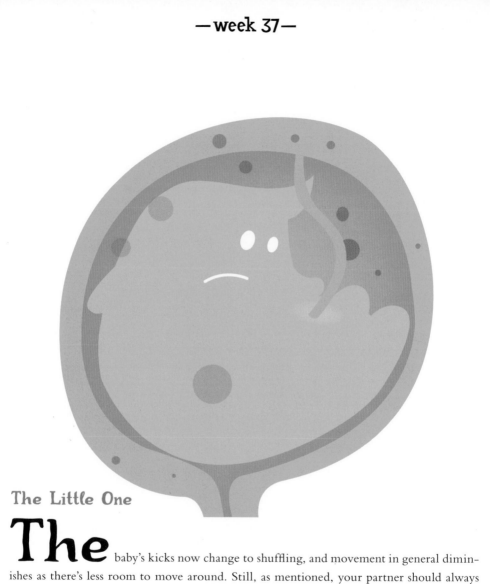

The Little One

The baby's kicks now change to shuffling, and movement in general diminishes as there's less room to move around. Still, as mentioned, your partner should always listen to her gut and speak up if something feels off.

The Big One

It's normal for a pregnant woman to get very nervous at the thought of being all alone when the contractions start. Suppose the entire show begins and you can't be reached? She may forgive you by the time you've had five children. But especially if this is your first, make sure that you set your phone so you'll hear it at all times. If you're used to switching it off during important meetings, you should now probably just leave it on.

The Little One

The little nails (fingers and toes) are often pretty long and sharp, and some kids are born with scratches on their faces. Some women even say they can feel the baby scratching them inside the womb.

The Big One

It's possible that you can't really prepare for birth. Every delivery is different, and you don't know what will happen. Stay out of the "epidural vs. natural birth" discussion. A pregnant woman always has the final word. If she wants an epidural, she gets an epidural. If she wants a tantric delivery, including esoteric breathing and yoga, don't make fun of her. A woman who can get herself into a meditative state during delivery is a genius. If she wants you to come along to pregnancy yoga, just go with her and join in. It'll make for a great story. Try to learn something from the breathing exercises. Nobody wants to see a dad having a panic attack at the crucial moment.

The Little One

The baby is now considered full term. The baby's head may be moving down into the mother's pelvis, or "engaging." The baby (somewhere around 20 inches) is ready for takeoff.

The Big One

Your
partner is probably pretty fed up with the whole pregnancy thing. The baby might come any moment now. But it could easily take another two or three weeks—requiring an almost inhuman amount of patience from the mother-to-be. Many of them will get pretty cranky. If any weird items suddenly appear in your fridge, chances are it has something to do with a tip from a friend or random passerby. Pineapple hearts, tonic water, and raspberry tea are supposedly good for inducing labor. If you tell a woman in week 40 that eating celery will get the contractions started, she'll eat all the stalks she can find. The good news is that semen contains a substance that can encourage labor, and an orgasm may do the same. If the doctor gives you the green light, turn on the Barry White. But be careful with her boobs—they're no longer toys (for you, anyway).

AND NOW, A WORD FROM YOUR VERY NEAR FUTURE

With the baby's arrival imminent, it's time to start getting your head in the game for life after baby. Just keep in mind: no matter how much friends and experts may warn you about the strain of life with a new baby, no one can truly express how difficult and exhausting it is. Additionally, no one who's been through it can recall the experience accurately, because stress and sleep deprivation during the newborn phase temporarily disable the brain's ability to record and store memories. Or so it would seem, anyway.

Internal Monologue

Expect everything to be different from what you expected, especially if this is your first child. You'll have a lot of confusing feelings: "So, this is my child. I'm supposed to love it—a lot, right? I don't feel anything. Literally nothing. Actually, I'm kind of scared. If I drop the baby, will it die? Oh God. If I drop the baby I'll be a total failure and my world will fall apart. Help! The baby's crying. What's wrong? If the baby cries, I can't sleep. That's not okay. Good God, is this the rest of my life? Never sleeping through the night again? What was that? A burp? Haw haw. Hey, the baby stopped crying. It's sucking my pinky. Look at him. He's crazy. He thinks it'll produce milk. And look at those little nails! Why are those little fingers so wrinkly? Is that all right? Hee hee, look at those little toes. Oh right . . . his skull hasn't completely closed yet, so his brain is right there. Have all the sharp objects been removed from the house? Oh lord . . . how long does it take for the skull to close? Can we have the baby with us in bed? If I put him in his crib, he's going to wake up, but if we bring him to bed, I might roll over on him in my sleep. Is the crib safe?"

On. And on. And on.

Panic

If you're left alone with the baby right in the beginning, you might feel some degree of panic. The same goes for your partner. If you get some crazy notion to go back to work one or two days after the birth, she will not be happy. So you'd better make sure that during the first few weeks you're around as much as possible to experience every second of parenthood—and to see your happy partner slowly change into a worried mother. Make sure that you two share the process of getting used to this bizarre new living situation. Take as much time as you can afford. Who cares? Go on walks together; talk about everything. (It feels weird, but you'll notice that other people find it totally normal that two young parents are walking behind a baby carriage.) Try to take as many naps as possible. It can take a couple of months before a man starts to understand what fatherly love means. And even though the process usually goes faster with mothers, it's basically the same deal. During this confusing period, it's important to be able to talk with your buddy in the trenches.

Hibernation

You know those scenes on TV where the nice young man walks into a bar and yells, "It's a boy!" and then everyone slaps him on the back and buys him a beer? Forget about it. That's fiction.

Your partner will most likely appreciate it if you stay with her at the hospital, and then at home, after the birth. Don't immediately invite all your friends for champagne toasts at her bedside, either, especially if it was a difficult delivery. Try to keep people away as much as possible during the first few days. Of course parents, brothers, sisters, and best friends will come by, but try to leave it at that. You can wait with the birth announcements. The later you send them out, the later other visitors will start coming by. And the later other visitors start coming, the better.

Storytelling

The first few days—or weeks—your partner will need to go through the delivery story over and over. First with you, then with her best friends, then her worst friends, and eventually with random passersby. At some point you'll know the story by heart. Just trust that this telling and retelling has an important therapeutic purpose. Also be prepared that several days after the birth, your partner will probably start crying all of a sudden, and will not be able to take it anymore. This is called the baby blues. It has to do with the changing hormonal situation after birth, and it's completely normal. Of course, for some women, the baby blues turn a deep shade of indigo. If either of you suspect postpartum depression, it's essential that she see a doctor as soon as possible for timely treatment.

Note: a new mother will be very happy with active washing machines, the smell of household cleansers, a spotless bathroom, and fresh bedding. The opposite is also true: a messy house will make her very unhappy. See if there's any way you can arrange in advance (like, now) for visiting family, friends, or paid help to keep things tidy.

The Little One

The baby's ready. Experts believe that the baby determines when labor starts by producing certain hormones, such as corticotropin-releasing hormone (CRH). In short, delivery is an intricate ballet of hormones and still has many unknown aspects. And while a baby at week 40 is technically ready to be born, a lot of babies have other plans.

The Big One

Same as last week. If she starts moaning, and does it again ten minutes later, and ten minutes after that, then labor has probably started. When she's screaming every five minutes for about a minute, it's time to call the doctor. These are the contractions that lead to dilation, and doctors estimate that in a first delivery, the cervix will open about a centimeter (0.4 inch) every hour. So there's definitely a ways to go. If she's lucky, it'll go faster.

THE DELIVERY!

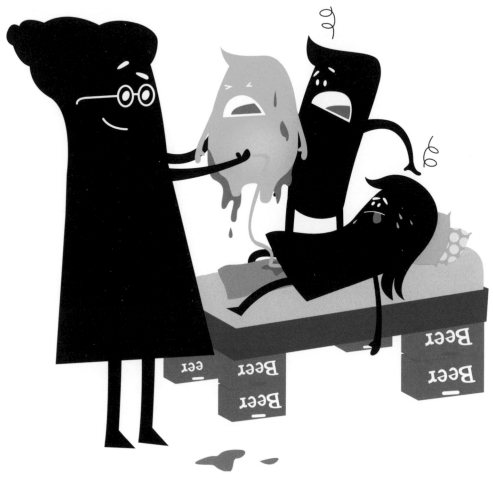

Most men think of delivery as being one event. That's incorrect. A delivery consists of several events. First there's early labor (including dilation to 3 cm), then active labor (dilation to 7 cm), then transitional labor (dilation to 10 cm), then pushing and delivery. Then, just when you think you're done, it's time for the afterbirth.

1. Dilation

Before the baby can enter the world, the cervix has to open up. In labor jargon, we call this dilation. When the opening of the cervix is 0.4 inches, they call it 1 cm. One centimeter dilation is a nice start, but not very impressive. The goal is 10 cm, or fully dilated. That means that the cervix can't open any further.

Splash

Somewhere during the dilation process, and sometimes even before that, her water may break. Splash, and the whole bed, or the new couch, is wet. (Note: often there is no splash, only a silent trickle.) Can't be helped. Amniotic fluid should be clear. In pregnancy books it is sometimes described as having a sweet, almond-like scent. If you smell something vaguely reminding you of that description, probably everything is in order. It may also happen that the amniotic fluid is brownish-black or greenish-black, which could mean that the baby has had a bowel movement. You should immediately inform your doctor about this, as it may be a sign that the baby is in distress. This is a reason to leave for the hospital (if you're not already there), so the baby's status can be monitored.

Membrane Stripping

Sometimes the water doesn't break at all. Sometimes the cervix doesn't just open. For one thing, there's a mucus plug in there. (This sounds kind of disgusting, and perhaps it is, but it also serves to protect the womb from external contaminants, bathwater salts, etc.) When the mucus plug is discharged and suddenly appears in the toilet bowl, this may be a sign that delivery has started. But it doesn't always come out on its own. If the pregnancy has gone past forty weeks, the doctor may try to get the delivery started by "stripping the membranes," which means manually separating the amniotic sac from the cervix.

Contractions

The dilation process can also begin before the mucus plug is gone, and even before your partner has labor pains. Gradually, the uterus squeezes itself to unzip the cervix bit by bit. This is called contractions. And once dilation begins in earnest, contractions hurt. At the beginning of a contraction it's not that bad, but the pain increases to enormous heights. If it's your first child together, you have probably never seen your partner suffer this much. She will make faces, and she may groan and scream.

At first, there's a substantial amount of time between contractions—sometimes even an hour. But at some point they'll start coming every half-hour, then every twenty minutes, and then every ten minutes. When they're coming every five minutes and last longer than a minute, the dilation phase has really started. And now the doctor will probably tell you to come to the hospital, if that hasn't already happened. (And if you haven't called the doctor, call the doctor. That's the phone number you have probably already printed a hundred times and that's stuck on every wall in the house. Probably, you have also programmed it into your phone several times.)

Pulling Teeth

So here you are, with a woman who sounds as if she's having a tooth pulled every five minutes without anesthesia. This is the moment to really show what you're made of. The trick is to be present—but invisible. Try to put yourself in the shoes of someone who's in a lot of pain, who doesn't know what to do, and who's trying to find relief. Your partner will be on the bed, moaning and groaning, and then, in between contractions, she might go to the couch to see if she can find a better position for the next contraction.

Contraction-Handling Paradise

You won't be a huge help if you're simply sitting there with a worried look on your face and tears in your eyes. Even worse, this kind of behavior will annoy her tremendously. So try to be useful. Help her think about contraction-handling positions and possibilities. If you're having a home birth, turn your house into a contraction-handling paradise. Turn up the heat. Run the tub with hot water, turn on the shower, prepare a few hot water bottles and put them on the bed. The less heat the body has to produce, the more energy is left for the delivery itself. Additionally, it's easier to relax in warm water, which supposedly helps the body produce endorphins, natural painkillers.

Pacing Around

Whether you're at home, at the hospital, or in a birthing center, try not only to be invisible but also inaudible when your partner is having a tough time with contractions. Don't start tapping your feet or pacing around. And don't be upset if your partner sends you away with a hiss. You'd do the same. When anyone is in a lot of pain, it's normal to want to be alone.

In fact, as long as your partner is groaning with pain, matters are not that bad. It means that she's handling the contractions. When she starts roaring like a lion, mooing like a cow, or grunting like a death metal singer, it probably means that she wants to push. If you're not sure whether she's groaning or roaring, then she's not there yet. You'll hear the difference. Your partner will get a deep urge to push the baby out, as if she needs to go to the bathroom really badly. "I can't hold it anymore," she may yell.

2. Birth

By now, your partner is howling. Maybe she'll look at you every now and then. If she wants you to sit with her, then sit with her. Depending on birthing positions (lying, squatting, hanging, standing, or sitting), you may get a supporting job. From now on, you're in a computer game. A role-playing game. And your part is that of a supportive yet unobtrusive figure who can take orders. Maybe they'll have you sit behind her as a counterweight, or hold up her thigh, if only to prevent you from standing there like a deer in headlights. As mentioned, your partner will yell, growl, howl, and scream as you have never heard anyone do before. The doula may sit beside her and coach her. "You're doing great, yes, push, push! You're a great pusher, wow!"

Apple

This stage may take some time,
or will at least feel like that. In
the meantime, many things will happen between those legs. There's blood and amniotic fluid, and a little bit of stool shouldn't bother you, either. And then, all of a sudden, there's a giant raisin about the size of an apple. It doesn't look great, but don't be startled. With every push, the raisin will come out a bit more. When the head doesn't go back in between

contractions, the doctor may shout, "the head's crowning." This means the worst is over. Now your partner only has a few more good pushes and the baby will be out.

At some point, they'll give the baby to the mother. A magical moment for everybody, young and old. The temperature of the mother's skin will adjust itself to keep the baby nice and warm, and this will make the baby all quiet.

If your partner has a C-section, your job will still be to play the role of a supportive and efficient order-taker. She may want you to hold her hand during the procedure, and you may even get to hang with the baby while the medical staff perform routine initial procedures on him.

Kiss

Chances are, whether your partner has a vaginal or cesarean birth, you will experience it all in a kind of shock, and won't know exactly what you're feeling and thinking. Try not to forget to kiss your partner and have a good look at your child. Most of all, try to remember what's happening. What the doctor is saying. What the nurse is doing. Let's be honest, this is a very special moment. And more importantly, in the coming days, your partner will want to go over this moment several times, minute by minute. During birth, not everything registers with her, and she may see things through psychedelic glasses. After the delivery, she'll just lie there like a dazed, love-stricken lump, and you'll be able to tell her many wonderful details later on if you pay attention.

The doctor may clamp the umbilical cord and wait till it stops beating. You will still feel the baby's heartbeat when you hold the umbilical cord between your thumb and index finger. You may get to cut the umbilical cord. It feels like cutting a chicken's cartilage.

You may be asked to remove your shirt and hold the baby to your skin. This is known as skin-to-skin contact, and some people believe it helps the baby to "imprint" your scent in his memory.

3. The Placenta

You've probably fantasized a bit about the birth, the monumental finale of the pregnancy. But in your fantasy, you probably forgot one big element: the afterbirth. When the baby is born, the party's not over yet. The placenta has to leave the body, and it's born the same way the baby was born. Including contractions.

And then, if everything goes well, after a few more pushes a kind of bloody-looking slab will come out. The doctor will lift it by its tail and show your wife. "Look, here it is." Don't be surprised if your partner stares at the placenta dreamily and says, "Ohhhh, that's so beautiful." During labor, due to the pain of contractions, endorphins are released, and they may have your partner looking at the world, including the placenta, differently than you. It all comes down to her thinking that, for now, everything is wonderful and beautiful, especially if it has come out of her body.

Hat

If everything went well, there'll be a kind of giggly feeling. Everybody will be grinning and acting as if the baby understands what people are saying. "You did a great job," or, "You didn't want to come out yet, did you?" Just try not to get too carried away. Male humor is usually not appreciated around the birth.

The baby will get a little hat and tiny diaper. Oftentimes, the doctor will have to stitch your partner up a bit. Eventually, she'll get a chance to nurse the baby. And when everything is done, you'll probably notice that you're kind of hungry. Because you haven't eaten for a while.

AND NOW YOU'RE A FATHER...

So this is what all the excitement was about. The baby is born. Now what!?

NOTES

NOTES